BRIGHT
IDEA
BOOKS

HOW DO
Wildlife
Crossings
SAVE ANIMALS?

by Clara MacCarald

Content Consultant

Kelley Stewart, Ph.D.
Associate Professor
Department of Natural Resources
and Environmental Science
University of Nevada, Reno

CAPSTONE PRESS
a capstone imprint

Bright Idea Books are published by Capstone Press
1710 Roe Crest Drive, North Mankato, Minnesota 56003
www.mycapstone.com

Library of Congress Cataloging-in-Publication Data
Names: MacCarald, Clara, 1979- author.
Title: How do wildlife crossings save animals? / by Clara MacCarald.
Description: North Mankato, Minnesota : Capstone Press, [2019] | Series:
  How'd they do that? | Audience: Grade 4 to 6. | Includes bibliographical
  references and index.
Identifiers: LCCN 2018018713 (print) | LCCN 2018021792 (ebook) | ISBN
  9781543541786 (ebook) | ISBN 9781543541380 (hardcover : alk. paper)
Subjects: LCSH: Wildlife crossings--Juvenile literature. | Habitat
  conservation--Juvenile literature.
Classification: LCC SK356.W54 (ebook) | LCC SK356.W54 M33 2019 (print) | DDC
  333.95/4--dc23
LC record available at https://lccn.loc.gov/2018018713

Editorial Credits
Editor: Megan Gunderson
Designer: Becky Daum
Production Specialist: Dan Peluso

Photo Credits
Alamy: Michael Hanson/National Geographic Creative, 22; AP Images: Jonathan Hayward/
Canadian Press, 16–17; Courtesy of CSKT, MDT, MSU-WTI: 25, 26–27; iStockphoto: Hailshadow,
8–9, 30–31, Lucilleb, 18–19, milehightraveler, 6–7; Science Source: Stephen J. Krasemann, 15;
Shutterstock Images: bunlee, 11, C_Gara, 12–13, 28, Enrique Aguirre, 21, Marina Poushkina, 5,
Skyward Kick Productions, cover (background), Steve Meese, cover (foreground)

Design Elements: iStockphoto, Red Line Editorial, and Shutterstock Image

TABLE OF CONTENTS

CHAPTER 1

TROUBLE IN
the Park

A family drives down a **highway**. They look for bears or **elk** out one window. They search for wolves or deer out another. They are in Canada's beautiful Banff National Park!

But the park once had a problem.

Its animals had a problem. Building

that highway cut the park in half.

Banff National Park is in the
Canadian Rocky Mountains.

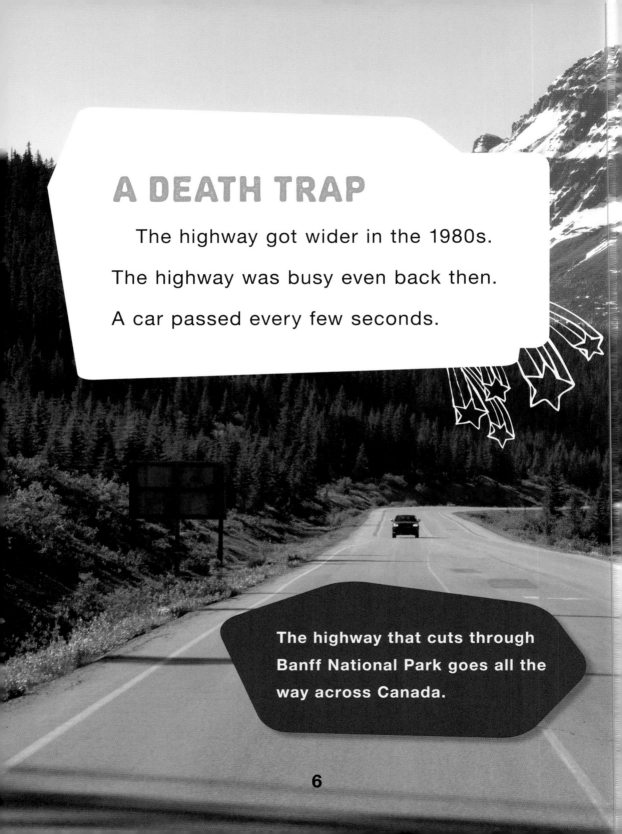

A DEATH TRAP

The highway got wider in the 1980s.

The highway was busy even back then.

A car passed every few seconds.

The highway that cuts through Banff National Park goes all the way across Canada.

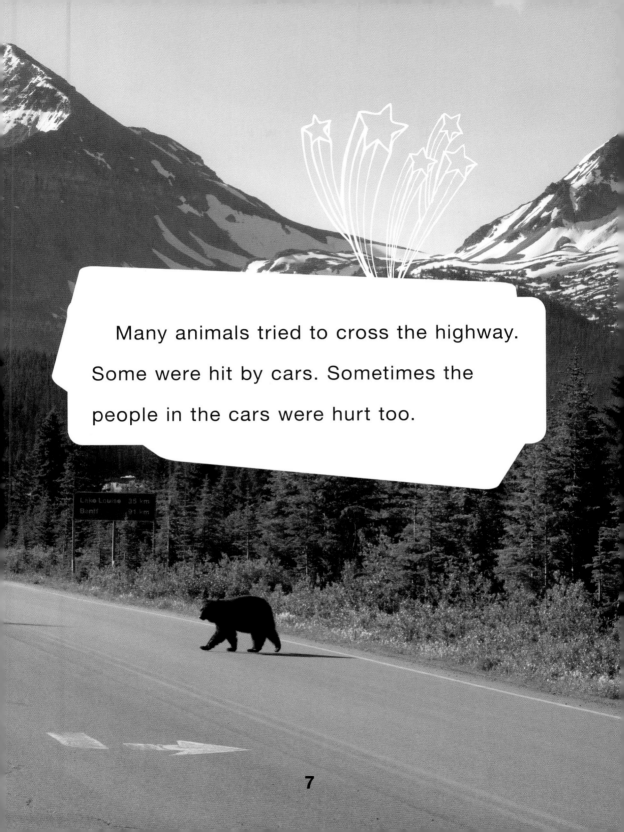

Many animals tried to cross the highway. Some were hit by cars. Sometimes the people in the cars were hurt too.

HELPING WILDLIFE CROSS

Animals needed to cross the highway. Large animals travel far and wide. They must search for food and **mates**.

That meant animals needed a safe way across. So people had to build one.

A small animal traveled across a rocky ledge in Banff National Park.

CHAPTER 2

GUIDING THE
Herd

The highway was great for travelers. But people started to worry about the animals.

Herd animals such as elk and bighorn sheep eat along the highway. This is not safe for animals or drivers. The animals are too close to the busy road.

People wanted to keep animals and drivers safe. But how would a **wildlife** crossing work? The idea was pretty new.

Bighorn sheep on the highway put themselves and drivers in danger.

FINDING PLACES TO CROSS

People had put up fences along the road. This meant big animals couldn't reach the highway. But they still needed safe places to cross.

Banff is home to thousands of elk.

Where would animals such as elk want to cross? People knew where they had been seen in the past. Maybe animals would want to keep crossing there.

MIND THE ELK

Elk are huge! Walkers and drivers in Banff must watch out too. Elk can charge if people get close.

CHAPTER 3

MAKE Way!

People started work on the wildlife crossings in 1982. Most were like tunnels. The highway formed bridges over them.

The first crossings helped large herd animals. But the park has other creatures too. People worked on new crossings for different animals.

People built underpasses for animals. They were pathways beneath the highway.

GETTING STARTED

Scientists looked for animals and their tracks.

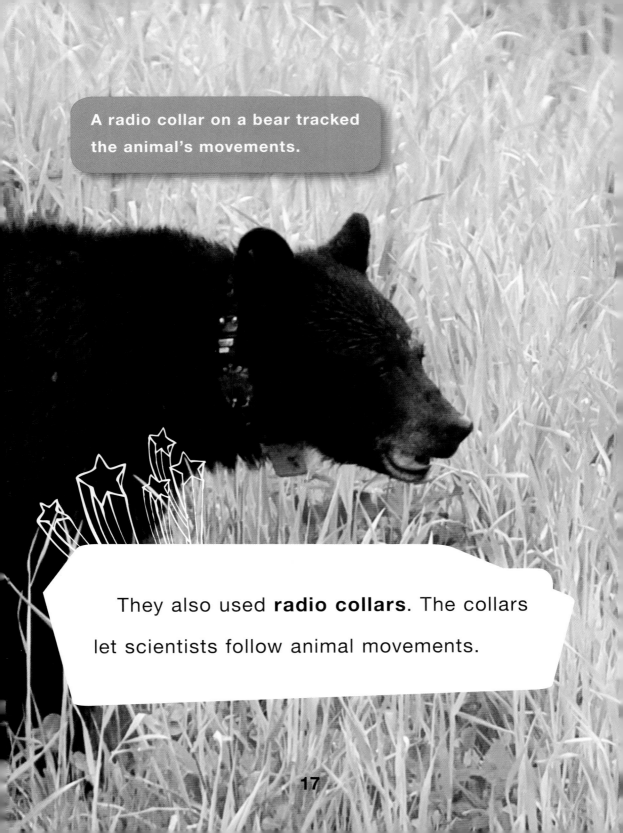

A radio collar on a bear tracked the animal's movements.

They also used **radio collars**. The collars let scientists follow animal movements.

Bridges over the highway blend in with their surroundings.

BRIDGING THE ROAD

People spread out the new tunnels. They built bridges too. Animals had lots of choices.

Two new bridges were built over the highway. Plants grew on top. The crossings felt like a natural part of the park.

CROSSINGS IN BANFF

There are 44 wildlife crossings in Banff. Thirty-eight go under the road. Six go over it.

CHAPTER 4

BUT DO THEY Work?

The new crossings made animals and people safer. The number of car crashes fell. Fewer animals were hit.

An important question still needed to be answered. Did animals use the crossings? Or did they stay on one side of the park?

ONE, TWO, OR THREE?

Scientists wanted to answer the question. They looked for animal tracks. They found tracks on the bridges and underpasses. They knew animals were crossing. But how many animals were crossing?

Prints are one clue that shows researchers animal movements.

What if grizzly bear prints were found in two different places? Were they from two bears? Or did the same bear cross in two places?

Scientists set up special wire at the crossings. The wire grabbed hair from passing animals. Scientists tested the hair. They could tell if hair was from the same animal or not.

ON THE TRACK

To learn more, scientists set up track stations. They made flat areas of sandy dirt on each side of a crossing. Passing animals left footprints in the sand.

Scientists also watched animals from airplanes. They also put cameras on trees near crossings. The cameras took pictures of movement.

CHAPTER 5

A WILD Success!

People studied Banff's crossings for 17 years. They noticed 11 kinds of animals crossing more than 200,000 times. Moose and bears used the crossings. So did foxes, beavers, and skunks. Even snakes and toads crossed!

HOW THEY LIKE IT

Scientists learned how different animals like to cross the highway. Wolves and herd animals like to go up and over. They choose bridges.

Black bears and other smaller **predators** prefer to go down and under. They choose tunnels.

Predators such as lynx seem to prefer tunnels.

CROSSINGS FOR TOMORROW

Banff National Park is famous. No other place in the world has so many wildlife crossings.

Studies there have helped animals in other parts of the world. People come from all over to learn. They go home to build their own crossings.

Wildlife crossings around the world save lives.

KEEP AWAY

Banff park workers want to add mats along the highway. What happens when animals step on them? They'll get a light zap. This will keep them from crossing at dangerous places.

Animals and people had to share the land in Banff. Scientists built animal crossings to solve this problem. They continue working to protect the animals in the park.

GLOSSARY

elk
a large member of the deer family

highway
an important road between cities or towns

mates
animals that make young together

predator
an animal that hunts other animals for food

radio collar
a band around an animal's neck, which sends the location of the animal to scientists

scientist
a person who studies the world around us

wildlife
animals living in the natural world

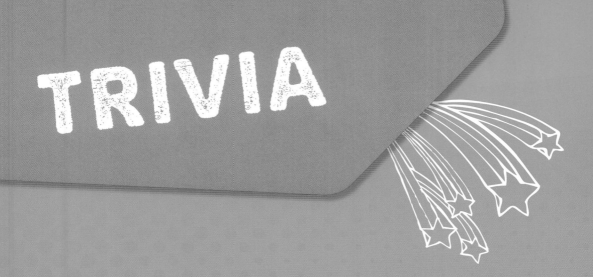

TRIVIA

1. Elephants in Kenya need to move. For a long time, they traveled from Mount Kenya to the Ngare Ndare Forest and back. Then people blocked their path with a road. In 2010, people made the elephants an underpass.

2. In Australia, millions of crabs cross Christmas Island at one time. They head for the ocean. They drop their eggs in the water before returning to land. The government put up fences and wildlife crossings to keep them safe.

3. The Netherlands has over 600 wildlife crossings. Animals such as deer and wild pigs use them. One crossing is huge. It goes over a road, a railroad, a business park, a river, and a place where people play sports.

ACTIVITY

What kind of animals live near you? Find a place you think animals might pass by. Maybe it's at your home. Maybe it's at school. Can you find any tracks?

You can set up your own sand trap. Ask an adult to help you mix sand with a small amount of mineral oil. When you press a finger into the sand and oil mix, it should leave a mark. If not, add more oil. Spread the mix over a small spot. Visit the spot once or twice a day. Did you find tracks? Take pictures of the tracks. Use books or the Internet to see what animal left them.

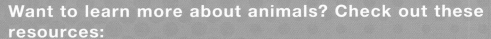

FURTHER RESOURCES

Want to learn more about animals? Check out these resources:

Goldish, Meish. *Gray Wolves: Return to Yellowstone.* New York: Bearport Publishing, 2017.

National Geographic Animals
https://kids.nationalgeographic.com/animals/

Find out more about Banff National Park here:

Parks Canada: Banff National Park
http://www.pc.gc.ca/en/pn-np/ab/banff

See more wildlife crossings here:

Earth Rangers: Caution, Wildlife Corridor Ahead!
https://www.earthrangers.com/wildwire/risk/caution-wildlife-corridor-ahead/

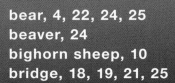

INDEX